REST UNDER PRESSURE

Hannah Orawua

authorHOUSE®

AuthorHouse™
1663 Liberty Drive, Suite 200
Bloomington, IN 47403
www.authorhouse.com
Phone: 1-800-839-8640

First published by AuthorHouse 6/12/2008

ISBN: 978-1-4343-7988-7 (sc)

Library of Congress Control Number: 2008902788

Printed in the United States of America
Bloomington, Indiana

This book is printed on acid-free paper.

Contents

Dedication

This book is dedicated to the Holy Spirit, my companion and best friend who has steadfastly been teaching and guiding me in all truths that have set me free.

I also dedicate this book to my loving family. To Cindy, who has worked side by side with me throughout the whole process. I extend this to her wonderful husband, Joseph, and their understanding children, Mbapelen, Aondohemba, Terungwa, and Nguemo Unongo, who allowed their mama to work with me.

I cannot forget my sweet brother Simon and my mother and father who instilled greatness in me at a very tender age. To my brother Ama, who always wanted the best for me in life: Your hearts' desire for me is granted by the good Lord.

FOREWORD

The purpose of this book is to provide proof that the grace of God is sufficient to help you through life's challenges without you giving up, and in turn to equip you to help someone else at a difficult time in their life. We are living in an age when God is using the personal experiences of people to bring hope and encouragement to the hearts of others who are facing storms of life in similar situations.

I convincingly announce to you that a new phase of your life has begun as you read this book. I am writing to tell you that God will step into your life and uproot every wrong thing that the evil devil has planted. He will heal every infirmity that is pestering your life. He will empower you above every lie of the devil that is terrorizing your soul. He will put your family together and fill it up with His peace and joy. He will pull greatness out of you and make of you the most awesome trophy that the world has ever seen. He will increase your days and brighten your future in a manner that will blow your mind. He is real; I promise you. He knows all about you. He knows where you are. He knows what is going on with you.

Through the ears of the spirit I can hear Him saying: I have heard the groaning, seen the struggle, felt the pain, the agony, the drought, betrayal, battles, the hurt, the mistreatment, rejection, false accusations, the hard labor, the stress, the deep needs, etc., of my child. I the Lord heal the broken in heart and bind up their wound (Psalm 147:3). All these things are illegal and must be deported back to hell today.

Are you stricken with a life-threatening disease? Are you deeply in debt and do not know how to come out? Has untimely death eaten up your life by snatching your loved ones? Are you lonely? Are you hated for no good reason? Have you been betrayed by your dear ones? Do you feel like all hopes are lost for you? Are you deeply discouraged? Do you think you have committed unpardonable sins? Is your heart worried? Do you lack peace of mind? Does everything you try to do seem to fail? Do you feel like God is so far away and has forgotten you? Are you struggling in any aspect of your life? Are you afraid of your tomorrow?

God is calling you into his rest. We labor so much and never give room for rest in our lives. You can rest in spite of the pressures of life. No matter your issue, God is able to give you the ability to rest while life goes on.

This book will bring peace and hope into your heart, for live testimonies of the goodness of our wonderful Lord and Father in my personal life in most of these areas are documented here for you. May the gentle Holy Spirit comfort, encourage, and bring healing to your heart as you read the doings of the Lord. You are richly blessed. REMEMBER THAT GOD USES THE FOOLISH THINGS TO CONFOUND THE WISE.

SECTION I

INTRODUCTION

According to Webster's dictionary, a covenant is a formal or binding agreement entered into by two or more persons or parties. It is a strong bond. It is an oath. God's relationship with his children is a covenant. In most cases, a covenant is enacted with a sealing sign. Jesus poured out his blood to seal the covenant between God and his children. You will understand the rest of God better if you understand who you really are.

It is important to understand that being a covenant child has many benefits. The redeemed children of God are those who have accepted the finished work of salvation, done by Jesus Christ. They have the benefits of divine protection, uncommon favor, divine provision, long life, divine health, etc., released over their lives daily.

Psalm 68:19: Blessed be the Lord who daily loads us with benefits, even the God of our salvation.

Chapter One

YOU ARE A COVENANT CHILD

You must realize that you are not ordinary, you are not of yourself, and you are a covenant child unto God. A covenant is a strong bond or an oath made by two or more people (parties). In most cases a covenant is enacted with a sealing sign. There are usually rules or laws accompanying or governing it for preservation.

As a covenant child of God, he has declared in the Bible to set a sanctuary amongst us. God is not referring to a building for sanctuary. He is referring to establishing a fellowship-link with his covenant people. Ezekiel 37:26: I will make a covenant of peace with them and it will be an everlasting covenant. I will put my sanctuary among them forever. God's outermost purpose for establishing this covenant is to bring humanity into divinity. It cost God the blood of Jesus to bring humanity into divinity.

The entire life and existence of man is based on covenant. The Bible commands us to teach our kids the truth. Deuteronomy 11:19: And ye shall teach them your children, speaking of them when you sit in your house, and when thou rise up. Verse 20: And you shall write them upon the doorposts of your house, and upon your gates.

The enemy (Satan) is afraid of the word, blood, and name of Jesus. The word must have free access into your heart. Your life must be filled with the word of God. Spend time with God; develop a hunger for his word. Do not rush and read the word of God out of guilt; God does not feed the guilty people but the hungry. The Holy Spirit is soul searching.

The word of God is a mirror. It will reveal yourself to you. It will clean you as you continue to read and study it. The word will also produce faith in your heart. Romans 10:17: You cannot pray if the word of God is not in you. The word of God will also give you victory over sin and Satan. Please I urge you to read the word of God daily, just like you eat every day.

Chapter 2

THE BENEFITS OF THE COVENANT

The work of salvation is a covenant. It is enacted with the blood of our Lord and Savior Jesus Christ; you enter into this covenant by accepting that you are a sinner who needs help. You acknowledge that Jesus died for your sins, and you are willing to accept him as your Lord and Savior.

Matthew 26:28: This is my blood of the covenant, which is poured out for many for the forgiveness of sins.

Another scripture on this is Romans 11:27: And this is my covenant with them when I take their sins. Jesus Christ instituted the Last Supper, and we are encouraged to continue observing it. As we observe the Last Supper the power of the body and blood of Jesus is made observable in our lives.

According to 2 Corinthians 11:25: In the same way after supper he took the cup, saying this is the new covenant in my blood; do this whenever you drink it in remembrance of me.

In Hebrews 9:15 for this reason Christ is the mediator of a new covenant, that those who are called (saved) may receive the promised eternal inheritance that He has died as a ransom (payment) to set them free from the sins committed under the first covenant. As a covenant child, you have the hope of eternal inheritance of God's kingdom.

Another benefit of the covenant is the spiritual ability to read, understand, and hide the word in our hearts; the word is life changing. Hebrews 10:16: This is the covenant I will make with them after that time, says the Lord. I will write them on their minds.

The favor of God is upon you because of His covenant.

Leviticus 20:9: 1 will look on you with favor and make you fruitful and increase your numbers, and I will keep my covenant with you.

Repeat this out loud: God looks upon me with favor.

Exodus 19:5: If you obey me fully and keep my covenant, then out of all the nations you will be my treasured possession, although the whole earth is mine.

How do you feel being called by God His treasured possession? Here the Lord is so clear. He says though the whole earth is His, you who have accepted the covenant of salvation through the priceless price of the blood of Jesus are His treasured possession.

Say this out loud: I am God's treasured possession.

Remember that a treasure is above ordinary. It is highly valuable and matchless. This reminds me of two sisters Lisa and Rose Ann. Lisa would carelessly leave dishes undone for a day or two, but one day when Lisa noticed Rose Ann taking out the china dishes to use, Lisa said to Rose Ann, "Please remember to wash the dishes when you are done; do not leave them in the sink." This came as a surprise to Rose Ann, so she said, "How come you are concerned about doing dishes today?" Lisa replied, "Those are china, not ordinary dishes. They cost about one thousand dollars, but the common dishes are just about five dollars."

China dishes are high in price but are of a good quality. Although costly, china dishes are still ordinary dishes, which are handled with care. Are we not, as God's children, worth more than china? We are so precious and dear to God that He has redeemed us with a costly price: the precious blood of His dear son Jesus Christ.

Deuteronomy 29:9: Carefully follow the terms of this covenant, so that you may prosper in everything you do. Another benefit of the covenant is prosperity. God has promised to prosper us as His covenant children. This scripture says to follow the terms of the covenant and live by it and you will prosper. If you embrace His word, you will join the psalmist to say all the ways of the Lord are loving and faithful for those who keep the demands of His covenant.

Hebrews 12:24: To Jesus the mediator of a new covenant, and to the sprinkled blood that speaks a better word than the blood of Abel. This scripture tells us that the blood of Jesus speaks better than the blood of Abel on the behalf of the covenant ones. This is why we must make use of the blood. Any time we apply the blood of Jesus, every wrong spirit disappears; and when we release the blood of Jesus in spiritual warfare demons fly.

This is a true story of Alex: As a young Christian, Alex witnessed two sisters praying and applying the blood of Jesus over a certain river where satanic activities were being carried out. Alex felt that this did not make sense; such prayer cannot change the situation in this river. But in the middle of the night, Alex ran out of his room and banged on the door of the bedroom of one of the sisters. All the adults woke up and Alex confessed that he doubted the effect of the blood of Jesus while the sisters were praying. But in his sleep, his spirit was taken to this river and the water turned to blood and as his leg was lowered into this river that was turned into blood it burnt him so badly that he began to plead and cry for help to come out.

There is power in the blood of Jesus, and as a covenant child, His blood is speaking for you. Remember that if God listened to the blood of Abel, how much more would He listen to the blood of Jesus that speaks on your behalf. The blood reminds every situation we apply it to that a covenant is made over this person.

Psalm 89:4: My covenant will I not break nor alter the thing that is gone out of my mouth. God cannot lie; He will not break His covenant with His people. The Bible is given to us as the law or rules governing the covenant, which is why you need to study it.

Jeremiah 11:3: The prophet declares: this is what the Lord God of Israel says: cursed is the man who does not obey the terms of this covenant. You cannot obey what you do not know; it is in your best interest as a covenant person to study the Bible. The Bible is the spiritual food that we need to live. Anyone who handles lightly the word of God cannot have substance in his spirit. Jesus says God is a spirit, so those that worship Him must worship Him in spirit and in truth.

Ezekiel 16:59: This is what the sovereign Lord says, I will deal with you as you deserve, because you have despised my oath by breaking the covenant. So let us not despise His oath, nor break the covenant. You are a covenant child, so live as such. If we stay in the covenant, every promise in the word of God is for us. The principles for the fulfillment of these promises are in the Bible. But if you do not study to know what the word says, there is no chance for you to practice it.

Psalm 50:16: The Bible says, but to the wicked, God says what right have you to recite my laws or take my covenant on your lips? Every transgressor is considered a wicked person. Refusing to study the word of God is transgression. This verse says if you are a transgressor, the promises cannot be fulfilled in your life. Do not forget the fact that it cost God the death of His son, who shed His blood to get humanity into divinity. God is looking for people who will live a life of total dependence upon Him, not independence from Him.

Chapter 3

GUARD YOUR HEART

(Your Mind is the Battlefield)

Your mind is the battlefield, so do not entertain negative thoughts. Every single minute there is a battle going on in your mind, good versus evil, truth versus lies, and light versus darkness. Every decision you make starts from the mind; the mind is the deciding factor in your body. That is why you have to be careful what you occupy your mind with. You must choose what you feed your mind with. Remember the saying, garbage in garbage out? The Bible says, as a man thinks in his heart so he becomes. You either lose or win a battle in your mind before you actually see it. Do not dwell on your past mistakes. Confess your mistakes and believe that God has forgiven you. Do not replay every wrong thing you have experienced.

The Bible says confession brings possession. Confess positive things. Remember that the scripture says that you shall have what you say. The devil brings negative thoughts to weaken our faith. Speak out loud when need be. Do not let the devil convince you that the negative stuff he put in your mind is actually true. Jesus spoke to the devil; use this as a weapon, speak out loud to the enemy (the devil), and declare the truth you know to his hearing. Think that everything that is good is prosperous to your soul and of good report, renewing to your spirit.

Doubt may try to come in, but remember that the just shall live by faith. If you are going through some stuff, the enemy (the devil) may tempt you to doubt God or be angry with God; but you must remember that your attitude determines how long you will stay in your wilderness.

God is a lot more interested in using your wilderness times to change you inside than in changing your circumstance in most cases. One example of this was the death of my mother. My mother died after a battle with diabetes, and I was devastated. I who had remained faithful to God had been let down. (Being human, that was how I thought.) How could God do this to me?

I eventually realized that Satan was at work trying to steal my faith and peace in God. Don't get me wrong. I did not readily realize this because I was so disturbed, but I did realize it and eventually won this battle. This battle culminated in me bringing my father and brother to Christ. Satan's plans did not bear fruit. I was lost in deep sorrow and mourning, and the Holy Ghost spoke to me one day and said that the devil had wrapped me with bitterness and sorrow so as to distract me from standing the gap for more members of my family to be led to the truth and be saved. This boosted me, and I shook off my mourning garments and began to witness to my family about the love of God in more magnitude. Shortly after this my dad got saved.

Be vigilant, for the devil may try to use what you are going through to make you sin. For instance, if you are going through some financial difficulties he may tempt you to quit tithing; but you need to remind the devil that as you faithfully tithe even at hard financial moments, God will by this tithe rebuke the devourer (Satan) in your life.

The truth of the matter is that even if we do not have everything we want, God still provides our needs on a daily basis. Psalm 68:19 says that we are loaded with daily benefits of free air to breathe, the benefit of shelter, the benefit of food, the benefit of clothes over our body. There are so many sick people as well as homeless people out there. Let us find something to appreciate God for each day. The fact is that we are not serving God for what we can get from him; we are serving him because of who he is: our creator. That's right, say out loud: God is my creator. Do not forget your root.

Be careful not to accept a false picture from Satan. He may try to make you think that it is because of sin that things are hard with you. But remember to put on the breastplate of righteousness; tell the enemy that you are made right through the righteousness of Jesus Christ. Do not feel bad about yourself; give yourself a break and lighten up. Appreciate who you are; God made you the way you are on purpose.

When Satan raises condemnation against you, tell him that you are bought with a matchless price, the blood of the lamb. And Romans 8:1 says that there is therefore now no more condemnation for those who are in Christ Jesus. Tell Satan that you are not his business; who and what you are is no surprise to God.

Put on the shoes of peace; do your best to walk in peace. Avoid getting upset because of your situation. Do not let Satan steal your peace and joy. God will give you the grace to keep your peace; the joy of the Lord is our strength. "And let the peace of God rule in your hearts." Colossians 3:15: Take the helmet of the spirit, which is the sword. The word of God is the sword. The word of God is filled with life. It is filled with power.

SECTION II

INTRODUCTION

In the Bible days according to the book of 1 Samuel 1:3, Shiloh was a worship center where people went periodically. Shiloh is not used in that context in this book. Though Shiloh was a holy sanctuary for periodic (yearly) worship, here it reflects a place in God that produces a worshiper. A worshipper lives a life of worship. Place, time, and condition have nothing to do with worship for a worshipper. It is a normal life.

This point in life envelops one with God's presence, which produces outstanding results. As children of God, Shiloh is a very important level to get to. The image of Christ is what the Holy Ghost dwells in us to conform us to.

Ephesians 3:19 says we should be filled with God. That is what Shiloh is all about. As you read on, you will see how people who sought this level in God came out with exceptional testimonies. It is God's will for every one of his children to be filled with him (his anointing).

According to the definition in Webster's dictionary, anointing is to put oil on as a sign of consecration. In the spiritual level, anointing is done by the pouring of oil. I Samuel: Samuel anointed David for kingship position.

Anointing can also be done by the Holy Ghost, which the evidence is a demonstration of power. Acts I: Jesus told the disciples to wait in Jerusalem until they received the Holy Spirit and power.

Acts 10:38 says how God anointed Jesus Christ of Nazareth with the Holy Ghost and with power and then he went about doing good and healing all who were oppressed of the devil, for God was with him.

If Jesus needed to be anointed, we all need to be anointed. It is only then that we can have the power to do the work God has for us to do. Delivering those who are oppressed of the devil requires anointing. We need to get to Shiloh to be anointed.

You can only work hard to achieve something that is of great importance or value. Having discussed Shiloh, a place in God that produces God's fullness in us, I want to show you how you can advance in the spirit to this level.

The Bible says ask, seek, and knock and you shall receive. To my understanding, asking deals with a need. In most cases we ask from God so often for material stuff, but if we want to get to Shiloh we must pass this stage. We must learn to ask for his presence to be actively resident in us.

Knocking deals with a demand. That is, to inquire we must understand that it is good for us to inquire how to regain the whole image of God. For in the beginning God said let us make man in our own image. That is what Christ has died to give back to us. So it is necessary for us to inquire how to get to Shiloh.

Seek means to go in search of or to strive for. I believe seeking deals with a deep hunger. When a person has a deep hunger for the glory and presence of God, they will do all it takes to get it. That is why you must implore these three steps to get to Shiloh, your rightful place in God. Do not settle for being a shallow Christian. The Spirit of God will help you as you seek him.

Chapter 4

SHILOH

Shiloh is not used in this book to refer to a city or town, but Shiloh in this context is a place in God that everyone who is a saved child of God ought to get to. Since the fall of Adam, humanity has been moving backward from God. Adam was fellowshipping with God daily. But from the day of his fall he began moving backwards and even hid from God.

Jesus Christ has come to restore that sweet fellowship, and David receiving this revelation declares in Psalm 91:1: He that dwelleth in the secret place of the most high shall abide under the shadow of the almighty.

Shiloh is the secret place of the Lord that is found at the mercy seat. In Exodus 25:22 the Lord says if you come to the mercy seat (Shiloh) there I will meet with thee, and I will commune with thee. Once you get to Shiloh the glory, power, fire of God resides in you.

A young shepherd boy by the name of David got to Shiloh, a place of restoration of God's image. He understood his ability to have dominion and also subdue his environment. He testified that he killed lions and bears, which attempted to mess with the sheep that he kept. David spent most of his time in the field with God.

When the prophet Samuel demanded that David's father bring out his sons before him, David was exempted, because his father and brothers underrated him. David handled rejection from his brothers, who saw him as incompetent to fight an enemy. Be encouraged in the Lord if you ever experience rejection or even if you are underestimated. In 1 Samuel 17:34–35, David said unto Saul thy servant kept his father's sheep and there came a lion and a bear and took a lamb out of the flock. And I went out after him and smote him and delivered it out of his mouth and when he arose against me I caught him by his beard, and smote him and slew him.

Because he had been to Shiloh he knew to take dominion even as a young boy. A man who has been to Shiloh functions properly as God's image. God uses ordinary people and ordinary things. A stone and a sling were ordinary, but a boy who has been to Shiloh (a man's proper place in God) raised them up, and God caused the impossible to happen; the giant Goliath was killed with a stone and a sling at the hand of someone who is living as God's image. God is no respecter of persons. Whoever seek his presence will find it. Age is no barrier; neither is race or status.

A woman by the name of Hannah knew that she needed to get to Shiloh and cause unpleasant situations in her life to change. You are created in God's image, so you exercise your authority whenever the need arises. Hannah was known as a barren woman, but when she took her place in God through prayer her story changed, so that she has this to say in 1 Samuel 2:5: They that were full have hired out themselves for bread and they that were hungry ceased so that the barren hath born seven and she that hath many children is waxed feeble.

Shiloh is not a building but a place in God that can remove the veil off your eyes, and your true identity is revealed and you function in it. Many people were in the temple praying, but Hannah with a broken spirit took a proper place in God. She delved deeply into her soul pouring out her heart in deep sobbing, and Eli the priest noticed her. There is a prayer that cannot be unnoticed. This kind of praying passes beyond screaming, shouting, and ordinary lips. This can only be seen from one who has been to Shiloh. Ephesians 5:18 says be not drunk with wine where it is excess but be filled with the spirit.

Guard against anything that would keep you from God's presence, for nothing is more important than spending time with him. Take time to be alone with God in prayer to adore and love him, to be quite and listen. A man who clings to the word or promises of God even in the worst times—God will not fail such a one. Never take the presence of God for granted or allow it to become commonplace.

In Deuteronomy 4:29: But if from thence thou shall seek the lord thy God, thou shall find him if thou seek him with all thy heart and with thy soul. Only people who seek God with the whole of their heart can get to Shiloh. Make yourself available to the Lord through intimacy, obedience, surrender, holiness, and worship. We ought to pray, but prayer is not something that can be rushed. We cannot expect God to respond by pouring out his glorious presence on an unprepared heart.

Say this prayer out loud: I command every cell in my body to go after loving God. I cancel every one of Satan's plans for my life and establish God's plans for my life today.

Chapter 5

HOW TO GET TO SHILOH

(Ask, Seek, and Knock)

Elisha had a great desire to get to Shiloh. He saw the power of God working wonders through a man who had been to Shiloh, Elijah the prophet. That created a deep hunger for Shiloh in Elisha. Elisha began pursuing Prophet Elijah to guide him to Shiloh; that is, to impart the anointing upon his life.

As Elisha followed Elijah, the prophet discouraged Elisha and asked him to stop following him. At Gilgal, Elijah asked Elisha to turn from following him. Elijah wanted to proceed to Bethel by himself, but Elisha persisted and went to Bethel with Prophet Elijah.

At Bethel Prophet Elijah made another attempt, and even the sons of the prophets at Bethel came forth to discourage Elisha's heart, but he would not let them. The devil can use anybody or any situation to discourage us from getting to Shiloh and getting deeper in God.

As Prophet Elijah was leaving Bethel he asked Elisha to turn from following him, for he was heading to Jericho. Elisha stood his ground to still follow Prophet Elijah to Jericho. At Jericho a different set of sons of the prophets came to discourage Elisha from following Prophet Elijah, saying that the prophet will be taken from Elisha very soon.

Elisha pressed on and left Jericho for Jordan with Prophet Elijah. At Jordan, Prophet Elijah parted the waters with his mantle, and the two crossed over to the other side of the Jordan. At this point prophet Elijah said to Elisha, "Ask what I shall do for thee, before I be taken away from thee." And Elisha said, "I pray thee; let a double portion of thy spirit be upon me." And he said, "Thou asked a hard thing; nevertheless, if thou see me when I am taken from thee it shall be so."

And it came to pass as they still went on and talked, behold there appeared a chariot of fire and horses of fire and parted them both asunder, and Elijah went up by a whirlwind into heaven. And Elisha saw it and cried, "My father, my father, the chariot of Israel and horsemen there of." And he saw him no more and he took hold of his own clothes and ripped them in two pieces. He took up the mantle of Elijah that fell from him and went back and stood by the bank of the Jordan. After the Jordan experience Elisha never remained the same. He pressed his way into Shiloh and dwelt there. He got the double portion of Elijah's spirit that he had sought. You ask because of a need, knock because of want, but you seek because of hunger. Elisha had deep hunger for a deeper relationship with God; he wouldn't let Elijah talk him out of it.

In 1 Chronicles 16:9 the Bible says the eyes of the Lord runs to and fro throughout the whole earth to show himself strong on the behalf of them whose heart is perfect toward him. A good lawyer wins a case by backing it up with evidence. The gospel's evidence is signs, wonders, and miracles. Jesus preached, taught, and healed the sick, cast out demons, raised the dead, and performed miracles. If the church preaches and teaches, but doesn't heal, cast out demons, raise the dead, or do any miracles, the gospel is not complete. The gospel is for the world; the doctrine and principles are for the church. Elisha persisted to get a double portion of Prophet Elijah's spirit. Elisha stayed focus in the spirit till he got the anointing. You must ask, seek, and knock till you are ignited with God.

Chapter 6

ANOINTING AT SHILOH

Genesis 49:10: The scepter shall not depart from Judah, nor a lawgiver from between his feet; until Shiloh come and unto him shall the gathering of the people be. Shiloh is the place or level at which you get ignited with the power of God. Once you get to that point his presence envelopes you so that you cannot help but remain there.

The presence of God in the life of man is all that you and I need. What do you want in life—peace of mind, joy, happiness, good health, wealth, blessings, assets? Just name it. All you need for all of these to come through in your life is God's presence over you.

Elisha, a great prophet who was wrapped up in God's presence (which brought his glory), died and was buried; the spirit of God refused to depart from his bones, such that a dead man was dropped over his bones and the man was revived to life. This fabulous account is seen in 2 Kings 13:20–21. This same Elisha in having dominion instructed Naaman the leper, a leader, commander of the army of Syria, to go wash in the River Jordan seven times, and at his words, Naaman came out a clean man. Elisha had been to Shiloh; the river had to obey. The Lord revealed to Elisha every secret plan that the Syrian king planned against Israel (2 Kings 6:8–12).

In 2 Kings 4:38–41, Elisha visited Gilgal, and the sons of the prophets had prepared a pot of pottage with leaves; it turned out to be that some wild gourds were among the greens, and it poisoned the food. Elisha ordered a meal and poured it in the pot of pottage, and the poison was healed and the people enjoyed their meal. That is the life of a man created in the image of God, who could take dominion and transform an ugly situation into a pleasant one.

In 1 Kings 17:21–22, Elijah, another great man who has been to Shiloh, stretched himself over a dead child, and instantly the child was restored back to life. This same Elijah had declared drought on the land of Israel for three and a half years, and there was neither dew nor rain. He also by his words multiplied the meal of the widow of Zeraphath. He had dominion over situations in his lifetime.

Elijah commanded fire down to earth upon his sacrifices at the contest on Mount Carmel before the prophets of Baal. Fire consumed even stones and water, because he was operating in his right image, which is the image of God. Jesus says the things that I do ye shall do, even greater things than this, shall ye do.

Elijah could subdue the earth; life and even rain obeyed him because he had been to Shiloh. Taking our proper position in God requires our willingness to stay connected to God. Right from the beginning God was coming to fellowship with Adam and Eve every day until sin came in. We can only get back to this mutual relationship if we strive to get to Shiloh. We need to get acquainted with God in order to demonstrate our true identity. Do not forget God is your life; outside of him you are dead.

In Exodus 14:21 we had the account of Moses leading the Israelites out of Egypt. Millions of people were in Egypt, but Moses had been to Shiloh and God placed the assignment of the deliverance of his people upon him. Moses never departed from God's presence; awesome miracles were done through him. A dry stick in his hand caused the Red Sea to part for God's people to walk through. With the same dry stick he stretched across for the waters to restore, and it happened.

Moses dwelt in Shiloh; he knew that the presence of God was the secret to all the mighty acts. At one point he told God, "If your presence does not go with us: I will not go (not move any further)." All the signs that demonstrated the greatness of God before the pharaoh and the whole of Egypt happened because Moses had been to Shiloh. God can use an anointed person as his instrument. Anointing comes as a result of hunger.

Joshua led the people of God to march around the wall of Jericho, and the wall collapsed. There is no doubt that Joshua had been to Shiloh; the presence of God was heavy upon him. In the image of God he took dominion, and a lifeless wall responded to his order. Every one of us lost it in Adam, but Jesus came to take us to Shiloh to recover all. Once we get to Shiloh, our true identity, which is the image of God, will be unveiled. Read this account in Joshua 6 and see what being to Shiloh can do in a man.

In the book of Esther, we read the account of a young Jewish girl who passed her way through into the heart of the king in her slavery status and obtained favor. I am talking about the king removing a rightful citizen woman from her queenly position and replacing her with Esther instead.

Remember that when you get to Shiloh, every situation bows before you and responds to your orders. Being a citizen of heaven gives you the authority to subdue the earth. It has never been heard in history before where a person is chosen in authority without their origin being highly considered. Esther was not checked out because she had been to Shiloh and everything had to agree with her. She wanted the throne, and everything had to give way for her to get there; all because she had been to Shiloh.

When the fullness of time came, Esther stood for her people. She exercised her right as the image of God to have control and dominion over the whole universe. She stood to say I have a right to the throne as the queen of the land, and my people have the right to live even in this part of the universe. And no one drew a sword against her or her people. Only someone who functions as the true image of God can do this; so we need to get to Shiloh so that our true identity will be unveiled.

We have the account of Peter and his companions who toiled all night but could not catch a fish in Luke 5. But when Jesus came by and ordered them to lower the nets, the Bible says that at his word they obeyed, and the waters had to release all the fish that it was hiding from the professional fisherman. Being to Shiloh has nothing to do with knowledge, fame, or experience. It has all to do with living in God. The Bible records that at the words of Jesus they caught so much fish that their nets were breaking and they called on other friends to come help them. All we need is his presence; for in his image he created us. Living without his presence is actually death. For he breathed his breath in you and me; now let us get ready and go to Shiloh. Then we can have a complete life.

The book of Acts 19:11–12 tells us of Peter and Paul. They have been to Shiloh. They carry the presence of God. They, such as when Paul's handkerchief healed the sick in his days, did miracles. The same applied to Peter; he was an image of God, and when he walked in the streets his shadow raised the dead.

Because Paul had been to Shiloh, in Acts 17 he said that in him we live and move and have our being. We are not separate from him; having this identity will help us to stay in Shiloh, and by so doing we shall subdue the earth and live in dominion as we were created to be. Paul still said our citizenship is not of this world.

As citizens of a higher level we have the right to have dominion. In the book of Romans 9, Paul calls us vessels of mercy, which God had afore prepared unto glory. According to Paul in 1 Corinthians 2:16, we actually have the mind of Christ. Some of us need to only get to Shiloh, and the very breakthrough, be it financial, mental, spiritual, etc., we are looking for will come forth.

The presence of God can cause the impossible to take place in our life; as such, it can drive out the satanic bondage in our life. Jesus says for us to seek first the kingdom of God and its righteousness, all we need is God's kind of life. Being in right standing with his laws and every other thing, the anointing, finances, good job, good cars, good houses, and good health, etc., that we are looking for can come our way much quicker and easier than we expect. The earth is the Lord's and the fullness thereof; his creation will obey you, if you obey him and live in his glory. Goodness and mercy, favor, wisdom, peace of mind, the ability to suppress stress will be our portion. A man who has been to Shiloh does not fail but rather amounts to greatness. All of this can only make sense if we make room for the Holy Ghost in our heart.

Going to Shiloh is what Paul was after when he said put on the whole armor of God. It requires action; you should put on Christ and a new nature. You don't have to be passive if you want to defeat the devil and live as a complete image of God. Stay active, get involved in the affairs of the kingdom, and get acquainted with God. Be on guard and recognize the devil when be begins to appear. Watch and pray. Wake up in your spirit. Understand your enemy (Satan). He is a liar, remember, and a deceiver and a thief. He wants you to feel bad and wallow in your mistakes; he wants you miserable and unhappy. He works through people, so be aware. He will always raise someone, somewhere to cross your path. Be smart enough to take your rightful place in the Lord, submit yourself to God, and resist the devil and he will flee.

SECTION III

INTRODUCTION

I saw Jesus by way of a revelation in a vision. It is so interesting how God is so close to us and yet we seem to feel otherwise. He lives in us. The Holy Ghost lives in us. In Ephesians 3:17, the Bible says that Christ may dwell in your heart by faith.

When I saw Christ in my night vision in the very chair that I sat in earlier in the mall, I was amazed. I was at the time seriously sick and was losing hope for my healing. Maybe you are battling a life-threatening disease or you are a single mom with the great responsibility of caring for kids. You might be on drugs and think that all hope is lost about your case. You may have a dream and it looks too hard to go about it. Read on and God will speak to you like he did to me.

God understands all these issues that you are battling. That is why he is calling you into his rest. In Genesis 2:2 God rested on the seventh day after creating the world, and he saw that rest was good (Genesis 49:15).

According to Joshua 14:15, even the land where the Israelites lived God gave rest. You must remember that rest is to cease work. We are so focused on our troubles and issues of life that we forget that God is concerned about this and God wants us to take a vacation from working so hard.

I used to be consumed with my troubles, struggling to get them solved. This kind of living was wearing me out. I could not enjoy the abundant life that Jesus has paid for me to have.

Lamentations 5:5 says we labor and have no rest. This is not God's will for us. As you read this book, you will discover that God is willing to do anything to bring us into his rest.

Are you waiting for all your problems to be solved before you can rest? Are you waiting for your kids to grow up and then you will rest? Or are you thinking of how to make a million dollars and then you will rest, etc.? These issues of life will never cease. All God is asking is for you to turn them over to Him. He will take care of them while you cease work (rest). Life will be fun and easy if we embrace the rest of God. Think about God giving rest to a piece of land. Your life is too tender to carry the burdens of life. That is why Jesus said, Give me your heavy burden and take my yoke. For my yoke is light and easy.

You need to turn your disease over to him and enter his rest. He wants you well and prosperous. I have been pulled back from near death several times. God is a healing God.

You may have some serious financial needs; in that case you are holding the right manual. Just read on and see how you can rest in even such a situation.

Life itself is a pressure. We are pressed by bills, jobs, family, disease, lack of money, etc., etc. Some people have the constraining influence of drugs upon their lives. Some are going through the constraining influence of gangs. To some people marriage is loading pressure on them, but all of these things do not have the ability to pressurize us unless we let them.

Habbakuk 3:16 says rest in the day of trouble. How do you do this? Simply turn your troubles to God and enter his rest. Stop trying to figure how and when they will be solved. God can perfectly and in a timely way do that. Worry will not help you. Your issues may be such that even money cannot solve them, but God will.

Chapter 7

I SAW JESUS IN THE MALL

For many years in my life, I used to worry a lot; bitterness was deep down in me. I would easily lose my temper over the most trivial issues. Though a saved Christian, I could stay angry for days once I was upset. This bitterness came as a result of the death of my mama.

Soon I was diagnosed with a chronic peptic ulcer. Not long after that the ulcer enlarged, and in 2001 my heart began to fail. My blood pressure was very high. I was undergoing treatment, but there was no improvement. I was in and out of the emergency room. I lost my job; I was getting weaker and weaker. I could hardly move around the house. At this point, spiritually I was weak. I could no longer pray so well. I depended solely on prayer lines from ministries. The ministry of R. W. Schambach was faithfully checking on me and praying for and with me. They also sent me faith-filled materials that helped to sustain my life spiritually.

I knew I needed a miracle to continue living. I fasted a lot and spent time reading the Bible. In weakness and pain I kept crying unto God to heal me. Isaiah 53:6 says: He was wounded for our transgressions, bruised for our iniquities; the chastisement of our peace was laid upon Him, by His stripes we are healed. This verse of the Bible became one of my daily dosages. I ordered many healing tapes from Benny Hinn's ministry. I surrounded myself with several other healing materials.

At this point, I had unpaid bills piled up and in the natural it looked like there was no hope for me to live longer. One day, I told my brother that I would rather die than continue in pain; I told him to get money out of my account and settle my bills. A couple of days after that, I asked my brother to take me to the mall so I could at least watch people and receive some fresh air. He dropped me at the mall and said, "Call me when you are ready to come home." I had not been out (except to the doctors) for several months. I tried to move around, but it was just too hard. I was weak and had lost a lot of weight. At the most I weighed one hundred pounds. As I sat on a seat in the mall, it felt like my heart was going to jump out, so I called my brother to come take me home.

In the night of this particular day, I was crying on my bed in severe pain with my eyes closed. And I prayed and said, "God may you please take my life, so I can die and get rid of this pain? It is too much for me to bear any longer." Suddenly I saw Jesus in a white robe sitting exactly in that spot where I had sat in at the mall. I said, "Lord, that's where I sat earlier today, where you are now sitting." I clearly heard in my spirit a voice say, "Yes, I want you to know that I was there with you in the mall on that seat, and you should know that you are carrying me, for I dwell in you. I have not left you. In any situation that you are in, any place that you are, I am there with you."

I used to hear people talk of seeing Jesus, but this was my first time having such an experience. The Bible says that even in times of temptation, God will not allow us to be tempted beyond what we can bear. God saw that I was getting weak in the spirit so He appeared to me to encourage me.

The next day after this fabulous experience I received mail from Marilyn Hickey's ministry. A letter was written to me from the ministry that said, "Hannah, myself and my prayer team were praying over a critical case that was sent to my ministry, but the Holy Spirit spoke through one of the ministers and said send this prayer point to one Hannah in Jonesboro, Georgia, and ask her to pray over the issue. We then went through our system and saw that you are the only Hannah from Jonesboro, Georgia, that partners with our ministry. I am sending this name to you but I will not release the issue; if you are convinced that this is of the Lord, do pray over it; if not, mail it back to us."

I was so surprised. I felt too spiritually low for God to do this. Marilyn Hickey's ministry was not aware that Jesus had appeared to me the previous night. With tears streaming down my face, I laid my hands on that mail and an unusual anointing came upon me as I prayed over that mail. I began crying and asked the Lord what He wanted from me.

He clearly spoke to me in my spirit and said, "I want you to know that you have got work to do for me, to touch lives, so you cannot die now." The next day I put the mail in the box and mailed it back to Marilyn Hickey's ministry.

I discovered that at our down moments, God's grace is truly abounding. I also realized that when we are going through attacks and pressure in life, God is still with us and He is aware of our condition.

He loves us irrespective of our circumstances. I realized that God does not want me dead, and He has work for me to do in this life. The devil came to steal my life in an untimely way but failed. This gave me great hope to keep positive, and my healing came in the process. One day I turned on the television and there was Gloria Copeland preaching on John 10:10, that the thief comes to steal lives and bring untimely death, but that Jesus has come to give us abundant life. This was another confirmation to me. I kept confessing abundant life over my heart, my immune system, and every part of my body.

I don't know what you may be going through, but remember that Jesus the good shepherd who has come to give you abundant life in your health, family, spirit mind, finances, your business, your job, and in your marriage, etc. Read John 10:1–18. You will discover that truly our enemy (Satan) is out to destroy every good thing including your life. But the good news is that the good shepherd on the other hand has come to give life and give it more abundantly in every situation in life.

Like I said, my healing did not come in one day; it was in a process. But the Lord did not only heal my physical body; He also uprooted the root of bitterness out of my life. You know that bitterness is poisonous; no one deserves to have that buried in his or her soul. I thank God for that deliverance. Today, I do not worry over stuff like I used to. I tell you, it feels great not to worry too much. I would not have gone through what I am going through now (if God had not prepared me) with hope and peace of mind. Having a good attitude at the time of going through the storms of life is richly rewarding, and it is also healthy to our souls.

The spirit of God asked me to write this book, for there are people who can relate to my life and find hope in God. For as you can see the grace of God has taken me this far.

I read about David and his experiences in the Bible. I also read about people like Moses, Job, Paul, Peter, Hannah, and Abraham, etc. All of these people were real human beings as we are, and they went through life situations and by the grace of God overcame.

Look at the account of Daniel and his friends, the three Hebrew boys: Hananiah, Mishael, and Azariah. Their lives challenged me. I have made up my mind, by the grace of God, that if God would document the record of His children who went through fire and hot water and came out with a good report, my name should be recorded as well. For He does not expect us to be perfect, but expects us not to faint in the days of adversity. I want you to know that God does not expect you to faint in the days of adversity. So hold tight unto your faith. This is no time to run away from God. This is the time to take the kingdom by force. The world is looking forward to your testimony. The world is looking for someone in their generation whom God has made walk through fire and who has not been burnt.

We are in an age where God is using individual testimonies to open the eyes of those whom the devil has blinded with false things. He is anointing personal testimonies to break chains off those lives that are in bondage and to bring hope to those whom Satan has lied to that their case is hopeless. Do not give up on yourself or on a loved one; God is still turning things around for the better.

Chapter 8

REST UNDER PRESSURE

Webster's dictionary definition states that REST is to cease working; to obtain ease or refreshment by lying down, etc.

On the other hand, pressure is the state of being pressed. Pressure is a constraining influence; pressure to conform socially. God has always wanted His people to enter into His rest. That is to let go and let God. When you lay down all your burdens upon Him, trust him with your issues and don't worry. He wants us to be in a relationship with him. He is concerned about us. He wants to be the Lord of our life. He is planning for us some good plans. But He needs our trust.

The rest of God is his Sabbath. In his rest we cease work and allow him to do the work for us. He loves us that much.

I use to be a right-now person. I never liked to wait. I also worried and panicked over any serious problem that I had to face.

This made it difficult for me to patiently wait on God. The Lord wanted me to stop this kind of life. Through a series of difficult experiences I have learned to enter his rest and keep my peace while I am waiting. God is the same at all times. He wants us to be like him, to keep our peace in spite of what we are going through. Jesus says come unto me all of you that have labored and are heavily burdened and I will give you rest.

Toward the end of the year 2006, I asked the Lord to give me a word for the new year of 2007. He simply said to me REST. I was so excited, I testified about it both here and overseas to family and friends. I structured out how to quickly sell three or four of my properties between the months of December 2006 and January 2007. According to my plans, I would make some money off of the properties, sit back, and rest. My idea of rest was not exactly the same as God's idea of rest, but I did not realize that.

By December 2006, I began to undergo pressure. I needed to appraise my properties so as to assess their value. The week before Christmas, I paid an appraiser $1,250 to appraise three of my properties. I went out with him to the sites, and he spent two hours doing whatever appraisers do and then he requested payment up-front in cash, promising me that the appraisal results would be available within the next couple of days.

I hurriedly paid him, eagerly anticipating that between then and the end of February my properties would have been sold. To this day, I have never again heard from or seen this guy. My money was gone. His phone was suddenly not working. I traced him to the address on his business card and ended up at a residence rather than an office, which was what I was expecting. A guy came out of the house, and when I said I am here to see Mr. So and So, he said, "We just moved here three months ago, and there is nobody by that name here." That was the beginning of pressure in my life.

I quickly raised more money and paid someone else to appraise my properties. This person did his job. I had preapproved buyers for four of my properties. The loan officer kept the first property for three months. Her explanation was that she gave out the title to be cleaned. In any case she ended up not closing the loan.

To cut the whole story short, none of the loans closed for seven months. Financially things were so tight that I became behind on all my bills. My properties were due for foreclosure. Even my phone service was disconnected. I had eight mortgage companies calling me. Foreclosure letters flooded my mailbox. Law firms began sending me registered letters.

My car was four months behind in payments, and all my credit cards were maxed out. My store accounts were closed. All I had left in truth was my faith. I felt like Job of the Bible. But the Lord renewed His mercies upon my life every morning, which took me through each day. I cried unto the Lord, and He instructed me to read the account of King Saul. Saul did not know how to enter into God's rest. He panicked under pressure and made some bad decisions. This denied him the establishment of his kingdom.

Saul was the son of Kish, a man of the tribe of Benjamin. The Lord sent Samuel the prophet (a prophet in Bible times was the voice of God) to anoint Saul king over the nation of Israel. As a king, Saul faced a lot of pressure. The Philistines gathered themselves against the nation of Israel. The prophet Samuel had instructed King Saul to wait for him in Gilgal for seven days. According to the Bible, Samuel failed to come within the given time, and he (Saul) had waited seven days according to the set time that Samuel had appointed; but Samuel did not show up at Gilgal, and Saul's army scattered from him. The fear and panic of a scattered army prompted Saul to offer a sacrifice without Samuel's presence. Saul acted against the words of the prophet Samuel at this point.

According to the Bible, as soon as he had completed offering the burnt offering Samuel arrived. Because this burnt offering was in defiance of God's will, Samuel told Saul that he had behaved foolishly because he had not kept the commandment of the Lord; therefore the Lord would not establish his kingdom upon Israel forever. In 1 Samuel 13:8–13, Saul had his kingdom cut short because pressure from their enemies and his own army caused him to take a step against God's instruction.

In another account in 1 Samuel 15:1–23 Saul was sent by God through Prophet Samuel to go destroy the Amalekites. Saul was to destroy this nation utterly and not to spare them, but to slay both man and woman, infant and suckling, ox and sheep, camel and ass. But Saul listened to the people and spared the good fat animals as well as the king, Agag. It seems that Saul did not know how to handle pressure, and he would always succumb to the voice of pressure whenever they put pressure on him. This is a bad attitude from a king and a leader.

When they got back from this battle, Saul confessed to the prophet Samuel, "I have sinned, for I have transgressed the commandment of the Lord and thy words because I feared the people and obeyed their voice." Saul claimed that he brought the fat animals to sacrifice to God; but the prophet Samuel said, "Has the Lord as great delight in burnt offering and sacrifice as in obeying the voice of the Lord?" Behold to obey is better than sacrifice and to hearken than the fat of rams. For rebellion is as the sin of witchcraft and stubbornness is as iniquity and idolatry" (1 Samuel 15:20–23).

In life we are bound to go through pressure, but be careful not to allow pressure to lead you to sin against God. The prophet Samuel again told Saul that because of his disobedience, God has rejected him from being king.

After Samuel died, the Philistines were preparing another war against Israel. Saul tried to inquire of God what the outcome of the war would be, but God would not answer him. Finally he decided to go consult a witch with a familiar spirit, who would evoke the spirit of Samuel. At the house of the witch at En-dor, Samuel asked Saul, "Why are you disturbing me from rest?" Saul related to Samuel how the enemies were getting ready to fight the nation and God was not telling him what to do. Samuel once again said, "God has departed from you because you continue to disobey the words of the Lord. And you and your sons will die in the war and the nation of Israel would be defeated."

The pressure of war caused Saul to sin against God again by going to consult a witch. God before now had instructed Saul to kill all the witches in the land, because God hates witchcraft (1 Samuel 1–25).

Another person who allowed pressure to mislead him was Aaron. Aaron was raised by God to help Moses bring the children of Israel out of Egypt (captivity). Along the way in the wilderness, God called Moses up to the mountain. While Moses was gone, the people chided against Aaron: They threatened to stone him. He could not handle the pressure and went on to collect their gold, with which he made a golden calf for a god for them (Deuteronomy 9:12).

I am writing this book at a time of great pressure from my life situations. I have studied and learned from these few examples that when the storms of life begin to rage, it is the time to calm down and seek God more than ever. We are in a world full of stress and pressure, but we need to ask God for wisdom in times like this. Are your bills, kids, job, business, marriage, sickness, status, friends, lifestyle, finances, health, etc., mounting pressure on you? Get into God; running for a quick fix may get you into trouble, because sometimes quick fixes are deadly. Remember that if you are not careful, peer pressure can cause you to compromise. Do not yield to it; read the Bible, pray, and talk to God-filled men and women you can trust. Know that nothing is too hard for the Lord, and He understands all that you are going through. He is with you in it. He can do the impossible. Does your condition look hopeless?

When Jesus got to the house of Mary and Martha, they had given up hope and were complaining because their brother Lazarus was dead. Frustration, despair, and unbelief were all greeting Jesus through these two women. To them, all hopes were lost, and Jesus was too late. But Jesus knew something they did not know. Concerning that very thing you are facing that looks like a mountain before you, Jesus knows something you don't know. As Jesus commanded the stone to be rolled away from Lazarus's tomb, the sisters said, "But Lord, he stinks, for he has been dead four days."

When Jesus said, "Lazarus come forth," something broke loose in the supernatural realm—where there was death—and life came bursting forth. Resurrection overthrew death. Where there was despair, hope showed up. Where there was the stench of death, a sweet fragrance came forth. Jesus spoke resurrection power into a dead situation. What is that situation you are in that looks dead? Jesus is the resurrection and the life; trust Him and He will bring it out from death.

The point here is not to allow the pressure from the issues of this life to control your life. Rest in God and he shall help you to keep your peace in spite of your circumstances. Remember that Jesus said that man is not made for the Sabbath, but the Sabbath is made for man. You are not made for life issues, but the issues for you. You have the God-given ability to control what you are facing. Your absolute faith in him can keep your mind at rest in the midst of pressure.

Jesus will give you rest and cause every dead situation, be it a spiritual, financial, material, marital, or health matter, to resurrect if only you will believe.

Chapter 9

REST

To a spiritual person, rest is a place in God that is not moved by circumstances but is dead to the false roaring of the devil. When you find rest in God, you can automatically praise and thank God in all things that you go through.

We are living in a very busy age. In this part of the world we are in such a hurry that we look out for a drive-through in everything that we do. This rushing spirit has thrown a lot of people into some health problems. God in his magnitude and love is concerned about us. He understands our heavy burdens. He is calling us into his rest. I used to run so much in life. Still I could not meet life's demand. This frustrated me for many years of my life. Today God has taken me into his rest, and I now have a normal life.

The prophet Habakkuk understood what rest in God was: In Habakkuk 3:16 he declares that I might rest in the day of trouble. Furthermore, in verse 18 of the same chapter, he went on to say: Yet I will rejoice in the Lord, I will joy in the God of my salvation. There is no one who has not gotten to that place in the Lord that will say, I might rest in the day of trouble.

The normal thing to do in time of trouble is to fret, freak, dread, worry, or fear. But when we occupy our rightful place of rest in the Lord, we too can say: yet I will joy in the God of my salvation.

You might say I need rest, implying no issues to deal with, lots of money, no illness, nothing to struggle with, etc. But incidentally that is not what rest in God is. As long as you are living, there will be issues to deal with; you may hardly be comfortable with everything in life. Remember that Jesus said we are in this world but not of this world.

In the book of 1 Samuel 1:10–18: So the woman went her way, and did eat, and her countenance was no longer sad. If you carefully read the account of Hannah, she struggled with her issue until she got to that place of rest in God: Even though physically her issue was still there while she was at Shiloh, her countenance was no longer sad. This is because she had prayed her way through to that place of rest. Her circumstance did not change in the very minute, but her attitude changed.

In Isaiah 14:3 the prophet declares, "And it shall come to pass in the day that the Lord shall give you rest from your sorrow, and from your fear, and from the hard bondage where in you were made to serve." Do not forget that every one of us has served Satan and had been in bondage before Christ came and set us free. We sorrow over issues at times, and we fear in some circumstances. But understand that this scripture says that it shall come to pass in the day that the Lord shall give you rest. This does not mean there will be no more issues to confront or no unpleasant situations; it does not mean no lack, or no devils to fight, but rather it means dropping the weight of all these issues at the feet of the Lord and ceasing to worry: Quit trying to figure out how the issues can be taken care of. Trust God with your problems and go on vacation. Be absolutely sure that God is working on it. And like Hannah, let not your countenance be sad any more.

Psalm 37:7 says: Rest in the Lord, and wait patiently for Him. While you are still waiting, cease worrying and rest. The scripture says He that keeps Israel shall neither sleep nor slumber. He is on your case day and night. He is making plans for your life. The Bible says He knows even the number of hairs on your head; rest assured that nothing that is going on in your life is a surprise to God.

As I mentioned earlier in this book, towards the ending of the year 2006, as is my custom, I asked the Lord to give me a word for the following year—2007. He clearly said to me REST. I was so excited that 2007 was to be a year of rest for me. I shared this promise with my local church and with friends around me and those overseas. As an investor, I had some properties on the market. In my mind, I figured out how these properties would sell and I would have money and no issues to worry about, for God had told me rest. As a matter of fact, I had three preapproved buyers for three of my properties.

I lost my money ($1,250) on one fraudulent appraiser, but by January of 2007 I got another appraiser, and the job was done. At this time, though, the loan officer took three months to clean the titles. At about the fourth month each of the buyers' credit scores had dropped. No loan was closed. Meanwhile, one of my properties was broken into three times. The second one was vandalized, and all appliances, commodes, all sinks, all mirrors, floor carpet in the master bedroom, window air conditioner, master air conditioner unit for the entire house, both front and back exterior doors, and one window were all gone. The third property was occupied, and the tenant who was behind on the rent for three months moved with no notice. One of the contractors I hired to fix one of the properties claimed to be working overnight. Little did I know that he had plans to sleep in so as to take possession of the property. I had to go through an eviction process to get him out.

By this time I was down financially and all my bills were behind. I began receiving foreclosure letters from seven of my lenders. I received a report on one of my properties for suspected illegal drug activities by my tenant. I gave him notice to move out, and two days after he moved, the house was totally vandalized. This went on for almost nine months. All my store accounts were behind, some were closed, and my cell phone was cut off. Bill collectors were calling me and law firms were writing me. I called the dealership to come pick up the car. People whom I owed were after me. My credit cards were maxed, and some were cut off by the companies.

I prayed the best I knew how and fasted long term as well as short term. I cried unto God. I murmured, I complained, and I asked God what my sins were to deserve this. I asked the Lord: Lord, you said 2007 was a year of rest for me. Where is the rest? I have more troubles than I can ever imagine. What is your idea of rest? I do not understand.

The spirit of the Lord then spoke to me and said, "I saw all these things coming against you. That was why I told you to enter into my rest. If you rest in me, I will take care of these things for you. For there is nothing you can do about these issues. They are beyond you, but if you rest (quit whining, trying to figure out, worrying, crying, and questioning, etc.) in me and give me your burdens I will take care of them." When the Lord spoke it was like a million pounds of weight was lifted off my shoulders. I also felt like a light was switched on in a dark room. His grace entered into me, and like Hannah of the Bible my countenance was no longer sad. I rested from intensive long drastic fasting; peace came back, and my joy was restored. With time, I reduced crying and thinking. It was not gone completely, but the peace of God remained resident in me. A lot of people might just discover this now from this book.

The Holy Spirit who is our wonderful comforter was awesome in doing his work in me. I asked the Lord for a scripture to hold onto. In my sleep one night, I saw a man who woke me and said read Psalm 138:7–8. I quickly grabbed a pen and wrote that down and went back to sleep. The next day, I opened my Bible to this scripture. Psalm 138:7–8: Though I walk in the midst of trouble thou will revive me; thou shall stretch forth thine hand against the wrath of mine enemies, and thy right hand shall save me. The Lord will perfect that which concerneth me; thy mercy, O Lord endureth forever: forsake not the works of thine own hands. I began feeding on this scripture; it was like my daily pill.

Only one of my properties at this time had rental money coming in. I knew that money was my seed, so each month I would pray and ask the Lord how to sow it to him. Because of this, the very property in question too was due for foreclosure. As of this date my car is behind for three or four months. Now even an old car can be repossessed if behind for two months. This is a brand-new car. I am the right person to have a title to it. I know that God has taken care of it; the Mercedes dealership had added all the money together and sent the bill for next month.

Only God can do this. I am under his rest, and I know that even though I am passing through trouble, his hand will revive me as promised, and I am positive that he will perfect everything that concerneth me. You and I are masterpieces (a beautiful creation) created from God's own hands, and he will not forsake us.

Another unheard-of testimony has already come out of this. Three weeks ago as I was downtown for Pastor Benny Hinn's partners' conference, I received a call from Omni National Bank to come over to the office. My loan officer said, "Hannah, we do not want to foreclose on you. All we are asking you to do is sign our property back to us." I quickly signed all the necessary papers, and one of the properties was taken off me—no foreclosure. I had never heard of it before, but all I can say is that God is perfecting everything that concerns me.

As a result of me entering the rest of the Lord, I have not lost my mind; with tears of joy, I offer praises to the great master perfector who is working behind the scene in my issues.

As God will have it, I am now assigned to minister in my local church and the sister church in another location. All of this has helped me to keep a good relationship and fellowship with my Lord. The Holy Spirit has been anointing me and renewing my joy.

Getting busy for God has helped me to not focus so much on my troubles but on Him. Not only that, but the Holy Spirit instructed me to write this book at this time. I want you as you read this book to know that the rest of God is comforting in spite of any situation. It is the point of unshaken trust and belief, that God has got my back.

The Bible says my ways are not your ways; my thoughts are not your thoughts. Humanly, when God told me to rest, to me rest was no problems or troubles, lots of money, fewer spiritual wars. I thought that if I sold four properties, I would rest financially for a bit.

The Lord caused me to understand that rest is to trust and relax; to quit worrying and fretting and not to struggle in my ability to make it happen. I learned to patiently wait for the Lord, knowing that he is in control and that nothing is too hard for him. And also to know that God loves me dearly and that whatsoever concerns me concerns him.

One day as I was watching *The 700 Club*, Terry gave a word of knowledge that there is somebody (a woman) who was not born in the

United States but is now here and is facing a lot of troubles, but the Lord is saying he is in control and she doesn't have to worry. I knew that was me, and it helped to build up my faith in my time of passing through.

God is not a wicked God. He did not bring any of this on me. But he is out to surprise the enemy of my soul and see me through each and every one of these issues. He is out to make a way out of all this mess for me. I know that God is out to make a trophy out of me and present me to the world. He is God. He can do anything. I believe as I rest in him that he is bragging on me to the devil.

I used to allow every problem in my life to get to my health. This was causing so much damage to my life. Thank God for opening my spiritual eyes to see a refuge (his rest) for my life. My health is now rescued, and I want to share this so that you will not harm yourself like I did.

Jesus wants you to enjoy abundant life in the midst of pressure. His abundant life is not conditional. The rest of God is not conditional. As a single parent you can enjoy God's rest. He will take care of your kids. He made those kids; he knows what is best for them. But you must trust him with them.

Your talent is given to you by God; if you turn it over to him you will experience his rest. He will cause you to excel.

Some people work two or more jobs to earn a living. God is calling you into his rest. One idea from God can put you into a better-paying job or business that will bring a financial breakthrough for life.

SECTION IV

INTRODUCTION

A divine encounter is a coming together with the power or presence of God. When we come together with God's glory, it transforms our life. The word of God says that for us to handle the power of God we must become new people. Ephesians 4:24 says put on the new man.

In the Bible days, bottles were made out of animal skin. When these bottles get old and worn out they could no longer hold wine or liquid. But Jesus says that old wine skin bottles cannot hold new wine. Wine in this context is used to represent the power of the Holy Spirit. And our hearts represent the skin bottles. We can only handle the power of the Holy Spirit if we become new creatures in the Lord. We must also strive to live a clean life. In order to hear from God we must make room for the Holy Spirit to dominate our heart.

Divine encounter gives us a divine revelation of God. This is what we need. God wants every one of his children to know him personally. You might be in a situation where no man can help you. You might even be in a place where no one can go in with you, but God will. Your knowledge of God will keep you in times when neither your pastor nor family can.

Chapter 10

DIVINE ENCOUNTER WITH GOD

It is so good to hear that someone has decided to give their life to Jesus, but this is just the beginning. Getting to the point of actually having or experiencing a divine encounter with God is what brings transformation. Divine encounter brings divine revelation of who Jesus really is. Your personal encounter will give you a personal revelation of who God is. This is very important, because you will need God be in the prison, courthouse, in the street, in the school, in the store, in the hospital, etc.

In the book of Acts 9:4–20 Saul and his company on their way to Damascus had a visitation from God. The rest of the people only heard a voice and saw a light, but Saul had a divine encounter as he fell to the ground and instantly lost his sight. But after his encounter, the Lord changed his name to Paul and also changed his life.

The woman at the well in Samaria took Jesus for an ordinary man, a Jew, but in the course of their discussion she had an encounter with her Lord and ran back to the city to testify how she has seen the messiah. A divine encounter comes with a divine transformation (John 4:3–39).

Mary the mother of Jesus had an encounter with her savior right from when the child was still in her womb. At the marriage in Cana of Galilee recorded in John 2 the Bible says that when they ran out of wine, this posed a hopeless situation. Even the disciples as well as the rest of the guests called on the host complaining that the wine was out. But Mary the mother of Jesus who had encounters with her savior knew that He (Jesus) controls situations, so she went to Him (Jesus) and simply said that they were out of wine. Mark the fact that Jesus's reply to her was, "Woman, what have I to do with you? Mine time has not yet come." But she turned to the servants and said, "Whatsoever He (Jesus) say to you do it." And Jesus turned water into wine right then. You do not worry or doubt God once you experience a divine encounter with Him. You know that He has power and control over situations and issues; so all you do is to turn to Him like Mary the mother of Jesus did.

Many people have met with Jesus, probably by way of introduction from another person or by reading some information about Jesus from some book or even the Bible; but you see, it is more than that. When you have a divine encounter with Him (Jesus), He takes total ownership of your life; He becomes your Lord indeed.

Chapter 11

NEW WINE AND NEW WINE SKIN

The Bible says faith comes by hearing and hearing the word of God. We feed our spirit with the word of God, and this in turn gives us light.

In Luke 5:36 Jesus told the parable of the new wine and the old wine skin; according to Jesus you are the new wine skin. His shed blood creates the new nature in us.

Now the new wine skin is fresh, tender, soft, and flexible, so it can be stretched or bent to any direction. Just as the fresh green leaf that is plucked from the branch, it is full of life, it is flexible, and you can fold it or bend it over to any shape or size. Christ has died to give us a new life such that we can be flexible for God through the Holy Spirit to instruct us and we receive and we are willing to go with God wherever he directs us.

When He guides us to show love, we will do so because the Holy Spirit is leading us; moreover the word of God has made us new wine skin.

On the other hand, the old wine skin is hard and dry; it is dead and cannot respond to anything. This kind of wine skin cannot hold the new wine.

If we compare this old wine skin to an old leaf that is dry, dead, and in some cases has holes on it, this leaf can easily break if you attempt to bend it. Similarly, the old wine skin has no flexibility.

Two things are mentioned here: The new wine is the outpouring of the Holy Spirit flowing like a river. This new wine has the ability to save, heal, deliver, and impact the knowledge of God in us. The new wine empowers us, anoints us, and enriches our lives with the awesome glory of God. As new wine skin (believers), when the word of God is poured in us, whether on the subject of giving, marriage, love, forgiveness, prayer, or fasting, we receive and obey; we are flexible in our spirit to God. That means that we allow God to stretch us to the direction of his choice and so we keep away from trouble and His blessings are poured upon us. The Bible becomes our standard of living.

The new wine skin is full of life, healthy, and can stand the test of time. The new skin believer does not fight with the word of God. They are humble and obedient, and they delight in the law of the Lord. They can fight the good fight of faith—why? Because they carry the new wine (filled with the holy ghost and power).

Just the same way I can fold a green fresh leaf with no struggle, the new wine skin believer is flexible to change as the Holy Spirit guides them and they are willing to do the will of their owner. Any time you begin to struggle with the leading from the Holy Spirit of God or God's anointed vessel, ask yourself this question: What type of wine skin am I? The old wine skin, which cannot handle the new wine, as the power of the new wine will cause it to burst? My question to you so far is can you stretch? Do not forget that God will stretch you.

In Acts 1:4–5 Jesus told the disciples to tarry in Jerusalem until they receive the new wine (baptized with the Holy Spirit). After the Holy Spirit fell on them the manifestation was great. For it poured on them like a mighty river rushing. They could handle it because the teachings they received from Jesus had built them up as new wine skin believers (Acts 2).

It says in 2 Corinthians 5:17 that if anyone is in Christ, he is a new creation. He has become a new wine skin (saved); he is full of life and power.

The new wine skin believer stays connected to God, worships in a good Bible-practicing church; at home, or even on the job, he lives in the presence of God. The leaf withers when it falls from the branch. The old wine skin cannot carry the new wine or be bent. It has no life; it is dead to the voice of God; it refuses to stretch to the leading of the Holy Spirit. As a prayer leader in the church, one Sunday morning as I was leading prayers my eyes were opened in the spirit. I saw the glory of the Lord descending down like dew. The sight was so glorious that I said to God, "Open the eyes of all these people so that everyone can see your glory." The Holy Spirit answered and said, "Not everyone here is prepared to handle my glory. If I release it on some people it will kill them because they are not cleaned enough to handle it." I wept, and that is why as new wine skin believers, we need to do the best we can to keep sin out of our life. Do not get me wrong. I am not saying we ought to be perfect. All I am saying is that we must keep our identity and live the new life. God sees if we do our best. We need to pray, study the word, fellowship with the brethren, and bear witness of the goodness of God to other people. We need to get addicted to loving and giving out love, sharing our possessions with those that are in need.

Remember that a new wine skin believer has a new mind, understands the Word (Bible), and has a new way of thinking; that is, positive thinking. He makes good choices in line with the leading of the Holy Spirit and the Word of God. He also makes new close friends who love the Lord, and they are themselves new wine skin (believers). He has the boldness to witness for Christ. You do not have a will anymore; the will of God becomes your will in every matter.

After I got saved, the Lord had to stretch me. I lost my former friends; they could not understand me. In the church, I met deep jealousy and resentment. I tell you the truth: Some folks in the church turn to envy the gifting of God in other people's life. But as a new wine skin believer, you have to love them. Keep a good attitude and move on with the Lord. Some felt that the pastor was giving me too much room to preach in the church. But the truth is that the anointing is of God, and no one can take away the anointing from another. I always say: People can take the microphone and stage from me, but they cannot take away the anointing. I experienced a lot of betrayal, but I had to stretch to love and serve in the house of God.

Chapter 12

I HEARD THE VOICE OF GOD

I got saved and filled with the Holy Spirit as a little girl. I worked so hard on establishing a close relationship with the Lord; he wrapped me with His love in a magnificent manner. But just like everyone else, I have been through hard moments and bitter challenges.

One of the darkest moments of my days was when my mama passed. This happened to be the first time I would experience the loss of a dear loved one. I had four months left before I graduated from college when Mama died of diabetes.

I had prayed for her and believed for her total healing when she was sick. She was saved and had the faith that God would heal her. After eleven years of her struggle with this disease she died. The good thing is that she died in the Lord. As a young single woman, this created a deep hurt in me.

I was disappointed in God; I was angry with Him. I cried and asked God why He allowed my mama to go. My world had fallen apart. Discouragement and depression crept inside me. A year passed, and I was still not free from the pain. I could not pray as before.

One day one of my big brothers gave his heart to the Lord; this brought joy and comfort to me. It barely was one year after he had been saved that he died in a ghastly motor accident. This was the brother I was very close to. He tried to cover up for mama in my life while he was alive. This devastated my life; I did not want to live any longer.

Though I had the call of God on my life, the ugly experiences of life caused me at this point to want to die. I did not think of my calling, for I was so consumed with hurt that nothing mattered anymore.

In the midst of this, one day the Lord spoke to me in the night and said, "Build me a school, an elementary school where kids will be taught my word and I will be planted in them while they are young." I said, "Lord, spiritually I am not on fire like I used to be, and financially, I do not have any money saved. My only brother who was rich you let die. I am only but a young single woman with no experience on how to run a school. I am not rich or popular. Who will allow their kids to come into my school?" I did not tell anyone, and I cried for almost a week.

One day a friend came to visit me, and as we were talking, she began sharing with me how a friend of hers had started a school. The beginning was so rough, but things changed dramatically as she persevered. I quickly remembered the dream that fellow shared with another concerning Gideon's victory that was to come over the Medianites (Judges 7:13).

I prayed that night and thanked the Lord for the confirmation. The next day, I went to the rest of my family and shared this vision with them. Their first question was: Do you realize how old you are? What experience do you have? Do you know the kind of project you are getting yourself into? I left with no one answer to their questions.

The Lord took control, so support came from family and friends financially, morally, and otherwise, and then Hosanna nursery and primary school was born. God healed me from hurt and also comforted me. The Lord raised me from nowhere to be the first in my family to be saved and the first in my family to own a school. I am here to tell you that God has plans for us; they are plans of good not of evil.

The Bible says eyes have not seen and neither have ears heard what God has in store for us. If God can raise up a little woman with a humble background like me to have a place in the society he can do the same for you. I cannot keep all of these from the body of Christ. I want someone to rise up in their faith and possess their possession today.

SECTION V

INTRODUCTION

In Genesis 1:26 God said let us make man in our own image. Man is inseparable from God.

According to Webster's dictionary image is a representation of a person or thing. It is a natural resemblance. Because man is God's image he is a natural resemblance of God. Every human being is expected to understand his identity. We need to live and be perceived as God's image. Colossians 1:15 says that we are the image of the invisible God.

Being a true picture of God, he wants us to prosper in every dimension of life. God is out to empower us to build wealth. Wealth covers money. We must understand that God wants to see our finances prosper. Your finances must line up with God's desire in your life, as you understand your proper identity.

A lot of times the devil tries to rob us of our proper financial life. As a result we begin to live under poor financial standards that even get us into debt. But from today debt must not dwell in your life. God disapproves of it, and so should you. Confront your debts today to get rid of them as you read this book.

Enter into God's rest; refuse to allow the pressure of debts to control your life. The moment you turn it over to God and get into his rest he will fix everything perfectly and you will live a debt-free life. You are a true representation of God. He does not owe so you must not owe.

Chapter 13

LIVE RIGHT IN YOUR IMAGE

(As the Image of God)

Now that you are debt-free by faith, maintain this identity, for this your actual image as a child of the most high God. Remember that you can only know who you are if you know who God is, because your identity begins in God. Put your bills in a stack, lay your hands on them, and say out loud: "As I sow, God will supply my needs according to his riches in glory by Christ Jesus. God is the source of my supply; therefore I have more than enough to pay my bills on time, so every bill be paid in full."

Do not allow your bills to mount pressure on you. Rest and relax in the Lord. He understands that your bills have to be paid. Obey the financial principles of paying your tithes, sowing in good grounds (Bible teaching and practicing ministry), and giving to help the orphans, the poor, the widows, etc.

Whatever you sow, you will reap; this is a spiritual law. When you sow words of doubt and fear over your finances, you will get exactly what you fear: LACK! Remember that life and death are in the power of the tongue. As you speak these words to your bills, you are sowing words of faith; avoid sowing fear so you will not have to reap what you do not like.

Galathians 6:7: Be not deceived, God is not mocked: whatsoever a man sow, that also shall he reap.

The scripture also say, as a man think in his heart, so is he. If you think that you are capable of paying your bills on time, living a debt-free life because God is your source, so shall it be.

In 2 Samuel 23:5 it says is not my house right with God? Has he not made with me an everlasting covenant? Arrange and secured in every part? Will he not bring to fruition my salvation and grant me my every desire? Sow scriptures that will yield some positive result for you.

Deuteronomy 28:2 says: God is the unfailing, unlimited source of my supply. My financial income increases as the blessings of the Lord overtake me. Another scripture, Psalms 1:3, says: I am like a tree planted by the rivers of waters. I bring forth fruits in my season; my leaves shall not whither, and whatsoever I do will prosper.

I want to cite some Bible verses that will encourage you as you read this book to focus on prospering even as God intends for you. Say these words out loud: I am blessed in the city, blessed in the field, blessed coming in, blessed going out.

My food basket is blessed, my pantry room is blessed, my health is blessed, and my family is blessed. The blessings of the Lord overtake me in all areas of my life (Deuteronomy 28).

When we give voice to God's word on a daily basis, the angels and the Holy Spirit work in arranging our prosperity.

They see to it that we are led by our spirit to be in the right place at the right time so that we will have the promises of God that we are confessing to be manifest in our life. Always remember that God has pleasure in the prosperity of his people, and Abraham's blessings are yours because of the abundance of grace manifested to us through Jesus Christ our lord.

Ephesians 4:23: My mind is renewed by the word of God; therefore, I forbid thoughts of failure and defeat to inhabit my mind.

Psalm 37:4: I delight myself in the Lord, and he gives me the desires of my heart.

I am filled with the wisdom of God, and I am led to make wise and prosperous financial decisions. The spirit of God guides me into all truth regarding my financial affairs (John 16:13).

Remember to read and say these Bible verses out loud, for the scripture says faith comes by hearing the word of God, hearing yourself saying what God said about you. Your mind will accept the message. Faith will come, and one day you will wake up and feel rich. Your feelings will fall in line with the word of God. You must understand that preaching of the gospel is for the world, but doctrine and principles are for the saints (saved children of God).

It is easy to get discouraged, but do remember that God's will for you is that of a blessed life. Some wrong things might have happened to you, but understand this: If, for instance, debts that are not your portion can find their way to sneak into your life, then you should rest assured that the blessings that are God's promise have a better chance to be fulfilled in your life.

Enter into God's rest, and financial pressure will not locate you. God will handle your finances better than you can imagine. Promotion comes neither from the east, west, nor south but from God. If you keep God out of your finances it will mount pressure on you. God will give you a divine idea to improve your finances. He alone can give you the wisdom to handle your finances properly. He is not out to take your money. He is after empowering you to make wealth. God wants to bless you.

Chapter 14

FINANCES

(As a Covenant Person, Take Authority Over Your Finances)

God is interested in your finances. He wants to see you prosper financially. When a person accepts Jesus Christ in his/her heart, such a person receives forgiveness of sins. In a similar way, such a person has to receive a complete financial breakthrough. For salvation is a total package of nothing broken and nothing missing. It is not God's will for his children to be struggling with their finances. Know what the will of God is for your life in every aspect so you will refuse the lie of the enemy (Satan). God wants you to be financially blessed. All you need to do is to follow his financial principles and the result will show forth.

Know that God wants you to prosper; 3 John 2: Beloved I wish above all things that you may prosper and be in good health even as your soul prospers. Find a picture that represents your heart's dream. It may be a picture from a magazine, newspaper, etc. Imagine it to be yours, blessed with the stuff that you would love to have. Have a deep look at it and picture yourself that rich and say these words out loud: "I receive a complete financial breakthrough in my life." The scripture declares in Psalms 37:4: Delight thyself also in the Lord and he will give thee the desires of your heart.

If you are in debt, exercise your authority as a covenant child of God and call your debts paid by faith. Consider the words of Jesus in Luke 17:6: If you had faith (trust and confidence in God) even (so small) like a grain of mustard seed, you could say to this mulberry tree: Be pulled up by the roots and be planted in the sea and it would obey you.

You might say, well, I have commanded but nothing happened. Remember that your word must be faith-filled for circumstances to obey: more so faith does not give up. You must speak of those things that are not as though they are.

One of the keys to this is your obedience to God as you live a life of obedience to God; circumstances are bound to obey you. Say this short prayer: Lord, help me to be obedient even in little things that you instruct me, so that I can rule over greater things. Everything I have, I am, and will ever have or be is in your divine hands. Now use your authority through the name of Jesus and speak to your finances and tell them to come in line with God's word. You can speak to the mountain of debt and see it removed.

Another thing to do while you wait for your finances to come together is to give a love offering to the Lord as a seed. Luke 6:38 says give and it shall be given unto you; good measure, pressed down, shaken together, and running over shall men give unto your bosom.

You have to give first, and then the Lord will cause men to give unto you. How he will do it I don't know, but his word say so. Also learn to give good measure back. Do not let your faith suffocate in the worries and stress of your mountain (of any kind). This attitude can make you look at God as a kind of cosmic vending machine, an insurance policy in a time of need. The fact about this kind of attitude is that it impairs our faith. It creates anger towards God; it severs our fellowship with God, who is the very author of our faith.

While I was going through financial crisis, my only one property that had good income coming in from the rent became my seed. For several months I collected the rent and prayed and asked the Lord what to do. Because I knew that the money was too insignificant an amount I needed every month to take care of my bills. I knew right away that the rent was my seed. I needed somehow to sow in order to come out of my financial situation. This made me to be behind on the mortgage of this particular property too.

This might not make sense to the human mind, but to the spirit mind I knew that if it was not big enough to take care of the problems, it was seed. And if I do not sow, I cannot reap. But I believed God that He would spare my property. After all, I was using the money to support His work, and as He promised (Luke 6:38), I knew he would take care of my bills. Abraham did not keep Isaac when God demanded him for a sacrifice; therefore, God spared Isaac and went ahead to make him the father of all nations. God will always multiply and give back to us more than we sow.

Chapter 15

CONFRONT YOUR DEBTS WITH THE AIM TO ELIMINATE THEM

Reach out in faith and take copies of your utility bills, mortgage documents, credit card bills, past-due bills, and delinquent taxes and write out on a sheet of paper the names of individuals you are in debt to, along with the amount; the balance on your car; loans from financial institutions that you owe; and lay them out before you. Say this prayer out loud: By the authority invested upon me through the name of Jesus Christ I call these debts settled in full! In Jesus's name debts I speak to you, be paid and be gone; cease to exist! I declare all debts paid in full, cancelled, and removed.

Debts, lose my address and never trace me anymore. God knows that we need to live life abundantly, and he has set it aside for us. Our vows, tithes, and offerings open the flooded gates of that abundance. Listen to God's heart's desire for you. Beloved, I wish above all things that you will prosper and be in good health, even as your soul prospers (3 John 2).

See, the word prosper means "to increase in every dimension." This means that God wants us to have abundance in every area of our life: financially, spiritually, emotionally, materially, etc.

God wants a debt-free life for you. You might have made some bad financial choices. God is not condemning you. He is willing to help you out of your situation. Worry, bitterness, and beating up yourself will not help you. In 2 Kings 4 the wife of the sons of the prophet whose husband died and left the family with debts was rescued by Prophet Elisha. God will rescue you from your creditors if you will let him. He is concerned about everything that concerns you, but you must accept his rest.

SECTION VI

INTRODUCTION

I would like to simply say that prayer is an act of talking with God. One of the ways we communicate with God is through praying. A lot of people think prayer is to bring petitions to God, but the truth is that prayer is not only about asking from God; it is a dialogue with God. It involves worship as well. God speaks to us during our prayer times, so we need to listen as we pray. Colossians 4:2 says to continue in prayer and watch. Do not slack in praying. Romans 12:12 also says continuing instant in prayer. We don't have to grow weary in prayer or praying. Being in a relationship with God requires praying.

In the book of James 5:15 the Bible says the effectual fervent prayer of a righteous man availeth much. We have been made in right standing with God through Christ. When we make our prayers effectual (that is, exercising power to produce the desired effect), such prayer can bring down the result we are looking for.

Remember that a fervent prayer is similarly a devoted prayer or a prayer with enthusiasm. The Bible encourages us in 2 Corinthians 7:7 to have a fervent mind toward the Lord. God expects us to be fervent even in loving one another (1 Peter 4:8).

As we apply the principles of God in every aspect of our life, we shall live at rest in a troubled world. God's principles work. They are given to provide comfort to us. Even in the case of sickness there is no disease that God cannot heal. Exodus 15:26 says: I am the Lord that heals you. God has promised to also heal our land if only we can trust him with it (2 Chronicles 7:14). Every disease known to humanity was placed on Jesus through the 39 stripes he received (Isaiah 53:5). If the doctors have given you devastating news run to Jesus and have your rest. There is nothing incurable with him.

In Josiah 14:4, the Bible says I will heal their backsliding. If you derail from the Lord just call on Jesus today and he will heal your backsliding. He is anxiously waiting for you to return back.

God might be calling you into a healing ministry to heal his people. Mark 3:15 says that he will give you power to heal the sick. All you need to do is say yes to his calling. As you read this book know for a fact that God is calling you into his rest. You just need to turn off your efforts and turn on God. He will free you from grief and worry.

Chapter 16

PRAYER

Prayer is an act of communicating or talking with God. We all need to pray in order to maintain a good relationship with God. Prayer is as important in our life as the air we need to breathe. As you pray, take time to worship God and do not make prayer to be only about making request for your needs. Bring worship into your prayer. Worship is the true fellowship that brings glory down at Shiloh.

One of the key things to help prayer work is to have a good strong love walk. If your love walk is intense, the devil cannot handle you. The secret to God's heart lies in love. Once you get to Shiloh you can love as a child of God.

Avoid jealousy in order for your prayer to bring result. Jealousy is a fresh act that kills the spirit. Do not be envious of other people or else it will lead to jealousy. Celebrate other people's victory with them.

Belonging to God is not a religion; it is a relationship. Let the presence of God dwell in you. God is seeking fellowship, abiding fellowship with His children. Those who abide in him receive supernatural strength to overcome jealousy. The key to this is the word of God. God's word brings His abiding presence into our lives. The result of prayer is always overwhelming. Prayer brings nature into order. Prayer can bring you into God's rest. Prayer is an act of spiritual warfare. Satan hates a prayerful Christian. But a prayerless Christian is a powerless Christian, and a prayerful Christian is a powerful one. You chose which category to belong to.

Chapter 17

EFFECTUAL FERVENT PRAYER

The Bible says that effectual fervent prayer of a righteous man avails much. I believe this scripture completely, for I have gone through persecutions because of my prayer life. I can testify that effectual fervent prayer terrorizes the devil and his kingdom.

One of the experiences I had as a result of my prayers is when I had gone to visit my elder sister. I had spent about five days when one day a young woman came to ring the doorbell at about 7 pm. As my sister went to get the door, I followed behind her. This woman had a switch in her hand. We exchange greetings with her, and my sister asked if she needed some kind of help. Her response was, "I have come to tell you that we need to have an undisturbed night starting from tonight."

My sister and I did not quite understand what she was talking about. So my sister said, "I do not understand what you are talking about." At this point, our next-door neighbor joined us. The woman clearly said, "You all have been praying and disturbing in this area, so I have come to tell you all that this has to stop."

At this point I said, "Ma'am, do you live around here?" She snapped at me and said, "I am here mainly for you, not your sister. If you love yourself, stop praying and disturbing at night or else you will regret it." As she was talking to me, she was waving the switch in my face.

I finally realized that it was a spiritual matter. My sister's next words to her were, "Do you know her (referring to me)?" To cut the whole story short, she left. Our next-door neighbor said the woman lived in another subdivision and she did not understand how our prayers could reach her. She did not hear us pray as close as her house was to ours.

We realized that the prayers were disturbing her in the spirit realm. It was not a civil case but spiritual; truly the weapons of our warfare are not carnal but mighty through God to the pulling down of strongholds. This happened in the southern part of the country.

Three years after the above-mentioned incident, I took a walk to buy some stuff that we needed for dinner one evening (in the northern part of the country) at a convenience store. On my way back, I noticed two young men walking fast to catch up with me.

For some reason I did not quite feel free in my spirit as I could faintly hear them talking in low tones. I quickly crossed over to the other side of the street where a man was standing outside the house on the porch. I stopped by this man, and those two young men looked at me in an angry way and proceeded. After a while, I took another direction and went home. I told my two friends (we were living together) what happened, we all concluded that those men were probably trying to rob me.

It so happened that two weeks passed after this incident, and one of my girlfriends and I went out on a walk to go visit another friend of ours. This happened to be another part of the town, and as we were walking I heard someone say, "We will beat the hell out of her for she thinks she has power."

I happened to turn back and asked, "Are you talking to us?" They both chorused, "We mean you, not your friend." Then my friend said, "Excuse me, do you two know her from somewhere or is there a mistake here?" One of them answered, "There is no mistake. She has being praying and disturbing our group, and we are sent to beat her (they were carrying large sticks); we are not here to play." They were both waving the sticks at me. I said, "The Bible says greater is he that is in me than whoever has sent you. If you dare to touch me, you will drop down dead as the Lord lives. For the Bible says touch not my anointed and do my prophet no harm." They cursed me out and left.

We turned from where we were going and came back home. At this point my friend said, "Don't you think these are the same young men that came after you two weeks ago?" I quickly realized that she was right. And I could clearly see that when someone is engaged in effectual fervent prayers, warfare prayer, such a one becomes a problem to the devil and his kingdom. Paul says, for we wrestle not against flesh and blood, but against principalities, against powers, against rulers of the darkness of this world, against spiritual wickedness in high places (Ephesians 6:12).

We have such awesome power in the person of the Holy Ghost. If we tap into Him, we will render the devil and his kingdom restless. As a young convert, I have always prayed and asked the Lord to make me a terror to the kingdom of Satan. When I discovered that the devil was so disturbed by my prayers, it encouraged me to keep fit with warfare prayers.

But my friend who went with me began crying and praying from the day after this incident for a couple of days. I noticed she was not her normal self, so I asked her why she was not taking it easy on the issue. To this day, her response challenged me. She said that the young men said they were not worried about her; their assignment was on me. That told her that her prayers were not a big deal to them.

I felt encouraged by the way she took it and wanted to come up higher in her prayer life. The attack on me aroused some kind of godly jealousy in her over her prayer life. So it was all worth it anyway. I would like you to be challenged to go deeper in your prayer life. Most Christians have forgotten about warfare prayer, but if you go back to the Bible in Genesis 2–3 the battle line is drawn. The Bible says: The serpent will bruise the hill of your seed, and your seed will bruise his head. So the battle line was drawn before you got here, let us not deceive ourselves and say there is no war to fight. Remember that while men slept, the enemy (the devil) came and sowed tares (weeds/kudzu). If you have been sleeping, wake up.

GOD IS THE SAME YESTERDAY, TODAY, AND FOREVER. (GOD IS MERCIFUL AND JUST.)

Some people think that because God is merciful, He overlooks justice. The eyes of God run throughout the whole earth beholding the evil and the good that people do. We cannot hide from God, for He knows even the thoughts of our hearts.

God is not requiring perfection from us, but He expects us to be honest to Him in all things. He is aware of our mess and weaknesses. All we need to do is come clean and ask Him to help us and deliver us from our weak points.

I remember back in my college days, the president of our campus fellowship came to announce one day that some money was missing from his room and that it was a donation that was given for the fellowship account. According to him the brethren were the people who came to visit him in his room, so the appeal was made that whosoever took the money should return it back. There was no luck to this appeal.

After a couple of weeks, he called the fellowship prayer secretary and myself (for I was his assistant) and said, "Go to God in prayer and inquire to know who is guilty about this money." The prayer leader and I went into prayers, and the Holy Spirit revealed to us the brother who took the money.

We called the brother in question and asked him, but he denied taking the money. This was on a Thursday evening. We asked if he was willing to allow us to pray that God who answered Peter in the case of Ananias and Saphira would equally answer us in this matter. He said that was okay.

We prayed and asked the Lord to reveal openly who was saying the truth in this matter. The following day, Friday, at about 12 noon the prayer leader came to call me out from my room. As I came out I saw a big crowd of students running towards the campus security office, and he said to me, "Run, let us meet up with them." He said, "I will explain when we get there."

We got there and he pulled me until we got in front of the crowd. To my greatest surprise, I saw the same brother we prayed with about the money matter. He had gone into some Muslim student's room while they had gone to the mosque at their hour of prayer. He stole some stuff from the room; unfortunately for him these students came back and met him with the stuff in his hands. They beat him and dragged him outside; the security officers saw the commotion and went and got him from them.

He was beaten so badly that there were bruises all over his body, and blood was coming out. They had torn off his shirt. When he saw me he looked at me and said, "Sister Ann." With tears in my eyes I greeted him back and left the scene.

To cut a long story short, he was fined for the stolen stuff, after which he was too ashamed of the public disgrace and dropped out of the university even though he had just one more year to complete his course.

It is not God's will for us to be put to shame, but He also expects honesty from us. When we lie to the Holy Spirit it is a grievous offense. I believe that if that brother had humbled himself and told the truth about that money, God in his infinite mercy would have forgiven him and would have also delivered him from that spirit of stealing.

We all have some little stuff that we are struggling with; let us learn to run to God and ask Him to deliver us, rather than running from Him. Like I said earlier in this book, God is looking for people who will seek dependency on Him and not independence from Him. According to 1 John 9, if we confess our sins, He is faithful and just to forgive us our sins and to cleanse us from all unrighteousness.

The Bible talks of the little foxes that spoil the vine. We don't have to be comfortable with our weaknesses, our bad habits, attitudes, soft spots, etc. They will hinder us from growing spiritually.

Chapter 18

HEALING

Healing is actually the children's (saved Christians) bread. These are Jesus's words. We dwell in mortal bodies that are subject to sickness and diseases, either as a result of bad eating habits, bad weather, or in many cases bad lifestyle choices. Some cases of disease and sickness are caused by sin, poverty, or old age. But you do not have to panic when sickness or disease strikes your body. Remember God's promises in this aspect. Isaiah 53:3 says that by his stripes we are healed. By faith we should take the word of God literally.

If hell would not rest until Jesus was crucified so that the scriptures will not be broken (fulfilled); heaven will not rest until you are healed so that the scriptures cannot be broken (fulfilled). God has greater power to heal you than the strength of that sickness you are facing.

The stuff we go through, be it sickness or diseases, are just attacks, but sometimes God allows us to go through them just to prepare us for healing ministry. I do not say that God places sickness on us: but I say that he in turn heals us when we are stricken with sickness and sometimes anoints us to use our experiences to minister healing to others.

Jesus said I go to prepare you a place. If the place requires some amount of time to prepare, how much more time does he need to prepare us for this place? He is coming back for a prepared people. Know that we cannot tell God what his responsibilities are. When you begin to counsel God—Oh no, Lord! You would have stopped it before it happened to me; why did you allow it?—know that at this point you are standing in a dangerous zone. Learn to give praise and worship in all situations, for this is the sole purpose for which you are created.

A good lawyer wins a case by backing it up with evidence. The gospel's evidence is signs and wonders and miracles, which include healing. Jesus preached, taught, and healed the sick, cast out demons (unclean spirits), and also raised the dead. If the church (saved Christians) preaches and teaches but does not heal, cast out demons, nor raise the dead, the gospel is not complete. We wrestle with forces behind the scenes.

One of the things that happens when sickness hits our bodies is fear. But fear is of the devil; do not entertain it. The scriptures says beloved, I wish above all things that you prosper and be in good health even as your soul prospers.

This is God's desire for his children. It is so clear that sickness comes from the devil, but we must not forget that in John 10:10 Jesus said that the thief comes for the sole reason to steal, kill, and destroy. Satan invades our health for this reason, but we need to remember that our Lord went further to tell us what His action towards this lie of the devil is in the latter part of this particular verse: But I (Jesus) have come that you might have life and have it more abundantly.

The spirit of God also spoke through Peter the apostle in 1 Peter 2:24: Who His own self bore our sins in His own body on the tree, that we being dead to sins should live unto righteousness; by whose stripe ye were healed. Now that we have established the fact that it is God's will for you to be healed, do pray and claim your healing, if you need healing. Receive it by faith and confess it with your mouth.

Once you pray, speak what you have prayed for. Do not focus or go looking for the sickness. James 5:15 says: And the prayer of faith shall heal the sick, and the Lord shall raise him up, and if he has committed sins, they shall be forgiven him.

Also know that in Exodus 15:26, the Bible says: For I am the Lord that heals you. And Psalm 103:3 says: Who (the Lord) forgives all your iniquities, who heals all your diseases.

The word of God is truth and solid to stand upon. God has spoken expressly in his word concerning our healing. Matthew 8:17 says that it might be fulfilled which was spoken by Easias the prophet, saying himself took our infirmities, and bore our sicknesses. Child of God, this is the moment for you to rejoice and receive your healing. Remember that God loves you dearly and cannot afford to see you sick.

I fell down in my room one Sunday morning as I was dressing to go to church. Incidentally, what looked minor at the time became major. I injured my right hip, and from the x-ray and the diagnosis of the neurologist, I had nerve inflammation. To cut the story short, I was in severe pain, and I had to ride in a wheelchair for the first time in my life. I was so ashamed and embarrassed. So many people in the store told me to get out of that wheelchair, for I did not belong there—it is meant for older people. I felt humiliated by life. I could not walk up stairs. I needed help to go into the rest room. I needed help to go take a bath.

The brethren and family members were around every single day to help me. I still held tight to the promises of God, confessing the word that by his stripe I am healed.

For a whole year, I suffered from this, but in his infinite mercy I am perfectly healed. I am now using my two legs, and I am living proof that God still heals. The psalmist says oh Lord my eyes are fixed. And that is my prayer: Oh Lord, my eyes are fixed unto you. He (God) has not failed me.

God has healed me of chronic ulcers, heart disease, high blood pressure, nerve inflammation, severe back pain, and severe toothache. I tell you the truth: God is a big-time healer. I am writing these testimonies to give people who are suffering hope. God is a good God; he is willing to set the captives free from any form of captivity that Satan might have placed on them. All you need to do is reach out to Jesus and he will rescue you, for the Bible says that the Lord frees the prisoners.

If you have problem with your health, enter into God's rest. He is your healer; he says I am the Lord that healeth thee. Take your eyes off the problem and set your eyes on the healer. Know that by his stripes you are made whole. The Bible says I wish above all things that you will prosper and be in good health even as your soul prospers.

As you enter into his rest the pressure of disease will not overwhelm you. Disease is illegal in your body and will be deported back to the pit of hell. I am a living proof.

SECTION VII

INTRODUCTION

This section deals with some living proof of the power and love of God. I want you to be encouraged as you read these proofs that God is willing to prove himself to you in your issue as well.

According to Webster's dictionary a proof is to verify the accuracy by an independent process. These testimonies are for you to verify the accuracy of the awesomeness of God.

Jeremiah 46:10 tells us that God of host has a sacrifice. We know that this sacrifice is Jesus Christ our Savior. The Bible talks about the sacrifice of the Lord's Passover in Exodus 12:27. Even as he willingly offered his life sacrificially for the whole world he is calling us into his rest from condemnation and guilt. The illustration of the sacrificial turkey is synonymous with the sacrificial offer of Jesus's life for humanity.

Chapter 19

LIVING PROOF (1)

I heard the story of a woman who was confronted with difficult times. She was stricken with life-threatening liver cancer. She lost her job, and financially things were really bad. Life was hard on her; all hopes were lost in the natural. She was badly in debt; at this point bills were left unpaid. One day she prayed and said, "Lord, are you still there? Are you still with me? If you are, give me a sign."

Later that evening her phone rang, and when she looked at the caller ID, it said, ALMIGHTY GOD. She was so afraid that she could not touch the phone to answer this call. The next day she summoned some courage to call back that number. Someone answered, and it happened to be a church with the full name of ALMIGHTY GOD CHURCH OF CHRIST. The name could not appear in full on the caller ID.

Somebody by mistake had dialed her number that evening. But then the brother who spoke with her asked her why she did not answer the previous day. She said, "Are you kidding me? How can I answer a live phone call from Almighty God?" I believe that God allowed the call from this church into her house at this time to encourage her. Do you feel like God has left you? Why not ask Him for a sign. He might give you one.

A lot of times when we are faced with difficulties our first thought is that God is no longer with us. This is the deceit of the flesh. God has promised to be with us even to the outer most part of the world. When you understand this, you will rest in him.

Chapter 20

LIVING PROOF (2)

Another incident is about a young girl who had done everything she could to get her father to commit his life to the Lord without success. She was very concerned about her unsaved dad, who would not open up for the Lord.

In 2001, when the World Trade Center collapsed, her dad left the house to go help out in rescuing people. He found a pregnant woman and helped her out of the building. She spoke to him and prayed with him to accept Christ as his savior. She also asked for his home address, since she was so grateful for the help. The man went back inside the building to find other people to help, but this time he did not make it out; he died in the fire.

His daughter was so worried about where her dad had gone in eternity. Several months passed, and one day the doorbell rang. As she opened the door, a woman walked in with a little baby boy. She said she was here to see Mr. Nick, who had helped her in the fire at the World Trade Center. The daughter explained that her father did not make it back. This woman in turn told the daughter that she led her father to Christ. And she had also named her baby Nick after the old man whom God used as the angel to rescue her from the fire. She said she had promised herself that after having the baby she was going to bring him over to Nick to see the other life he had saved.

At this point, the daughter was comforted, hearing that her dad made the decision for Christ before he died.

These are true stories that are present-day proof to us that God works in mysterious ways. God loves us so much that He gave His only begotten son for us. Are you confused about anything? Turn it over to the Lord and rest. He will reveal everything to you at the fullness of time. But you must learn how to rest in him and trust him with your troubles.

Maybe you are concerned about a loved one: Enter God's rest and watch him take care of that person. God loves such a person more than you do, and he is the owner of that life. The rest of God is burden removing. His rest gives peace and healthy life. God is willing to bring his kingdom down in your life right here on earth.

Chapter 21

A SACRIFICIAL TURKEY

As advanced as America is, I do not think there is any person who will be bold enough to handle this illustration that the Holy Spirit dropped in my spirit about the Lamb of God that willingly laid down His life for us.

You can agree with me that Thanksgiving is celebrated with turkey in this country. Who will have the guts if on the eve of Thanksgiving day, their doorbell rang, and as they opened the door, a turkey stood there with a bag of groceries containing stuffing, collard greens, salt, vegetable cooking oil, dressing, spices, etc., hanging on its wings? If the turkey said to the homeowner I have come so you can kill me for your Thanksgiving dinner for your family. Would anyone be bold enough to snatch that turkey inside and go kill and cook?

In Luke 22:7 to the end, the Bible says: Then came the day of unleavened bread, when the Passover must be killed. Remember that Jesus is the Passover to be killed. The disciples asked Him, where do you want us to prepare for the pass over? Jesus sent Peter and John to go book the room for the Passover. Jesus knew that was when He would have the Last Supper with them and later be killed.

As the Lamb who willingly laid down His life for humanity, He got for Himself the ass to ride on into Jerusalem willingly; chose the building; chose the furniture to sit on, etc. The Lamb of God as a pure sacrifice made provision for everything necessary for the process towards His sacrificial death for you and me. And at the set time when the soldiers came to arrest Him, He asked them, "Who are you looking for?" And they answered, "Jesus of Nazareth." And He said, "I am He," and they all fell down. When they got up He still asked them, "Who are you looking for?" They answered Jesus of Nazareth. He told them for the second time, "I am He. Take me, but let these ones (referring to His disciples) go." And they took Him.

I promise you that there is nothing God can keep from us, if it is good for us. I had a deeper revelation of Easter from this revelation, and it had a profound impact in my life in a new way. His goodness has taken me this far, and writing this book is proof of His goodness. For if He can give His life for me, what else can He withhold from me?

God is willing to do outstanding things in your life. I hope that my personal testimony will stir up faith in your life to open up for the Lord so He can pull out all the potentials He has buried in you right before you were born. Yes, God can use the foolish things of the world to confound the wise.

Remember that for every drastic trial you go through there is a bigger comfort awaiting you at the other side. God sometimes deliberately lets us get into a storm, for the storm will always cause us to seek Him more. Remember that the storm will not envelop you because God wants to develop you.

You must also know that passing through the storm does not mean that God is angry with you; it may be that God is bragging on you to the devil. God wants to prove to the devil that you are original and not counterfeit. A counterfeit will fade, change, wear out, etc., in the face of storms, hardship, troubled times, difficulties, etc. But the original will pass through fire and come out with no smell of smoke. God may lead you through the path you may not want to go, but He will certainly take you to the place you need to be.

Seek God for yourself. Know that information will bring you to, but revelation will bring you through. Once you have a revelation of God's rest you will take a vacation from handling your affairs. You will begin to enjoy the abundant life that Jesus died for you to have.

Chapter 22

CONCLUSION

Here is God using an ordinary young woman to do the impossible. This was a divine proof in my life that God is with me. Do you have some uncomfortable experiences that the devil is using to lie to you that God does not love you and that nothing good can come out of your life? Have you lost a loved one and feel like there is no meaning in life anymore? Do you have a dream that looks like it is too big for you to handle?

Have you lost everything and feel like Job of the Bible? Are you under such financial drought that you are barely making it from each day to the other? Are you so much in debt that you can hardly sleep at night? Have you been stricken by some disease that is life threatening? Are you so sick but yet do not have insurance to go see a doctor? Have you received notice of foreclosure of your home? Are you so behind on your car note that you go to bed some nights not being sure you will wake up and still see your car in the driveway?

If you answer yes to any of this questions, get up like Hannah of the Bible and let not your heart be sorrowful or sad. Shake off the spirit of discouragement and heaviness. I am a living witness that our daddy (God) will visit your situation, and it will blow your mind what His comfort will be to your soul. I am a living proof. I have gone through some of these and beyond but I am still here.

God knows that you cannot handle the drug addiction of your child. He knows about your unfaithful partner. He is aware of your test result. God is aware of the fact that you need a life partner. Jesus sees your bank account. Our Lord knows that you are a single parent. God knows that you need another car. He is aware that your paycheck cannot sustain your household. That is why he is calling you into his rest. You have labored enough; it is time to let go and let God.

That we live in a world full of pressure is a fact. Know that fact cannot set you free, but truth will. It has been a journey of rest. So far you can agree with me that you can rest while life goes on. Remember that Jesus is saying do not go through life by yourself. It is too hard. He did not design you for that. You are designed to rest. That means he is in control, in charge, and in power.

PRAYER OF SALVATION

If you have not given your life to the Lord Jesus please repeat this prayer from your heart. God bless you as you do so.

LORD JESUS I AM A SINNER. I COME TO YOU TODAY. FORGIVE MY SINS. WASH ME WITH YOUR BLOOD. COME INTO MY HEART, FOR I KNOW THAT YOU DIED FOR ME. THANK YOU FOR SAVING ME, LORD. GIVE ME THE GRACE TO LIVE FOR YOU ALL THE DAYS OF MY LIFE.

About the Author

Hannah A. Orawua is a woman of faith. She has passion to motivate believers to get deeper in the Lord, as well as a deep hunger for souls to be reconciled to the Lord.

God has healed her of chronic ulcer, heart disease, nerve inflammation, and severe back pain. She has also passed through financial drought and every imaginable physical and mental pressure into the rest of God. She is a writer, teacher, and preacher of the word.

Hannah is the founder of a highly spiritually based standard elementary school (Hosanna International School) in Nigeria, West Africa, where kids are introduced to the saving knowledge of the Lord while they are young.

She has another powerful book on the way. Watch out and don't miss it. It is another life-changing message from God.